INVISIBLE
Threads

INVISIBLE
Threads

My voice has been silenced forever

Shobha Kulkarni

PARTRIDGE

To order additional copies of this book, contact
Partridge India
000 800 10062 62
orders.india@partridgepublishing.com

www.partridgepublishing.com/india

Contents

To Mother Earth –
My source of Inspiration

The higher the branches grow, the lighter they become, the ornate leaves decorate them and then the dance of heavenly music starts. The branches sway with the wind and bend to the Supreme will.

Foreword

Every poet has his/her own way of thinking. He develops his own philosophy.His vision of looking towards the world is different.Herein the physical and metaphysical vision is clear and transparent.Most of the poems are centred around 'I'and 'me'.The subjective impressions, more or less, are very significant-

> you tapped on my window pane
> I opened the door
> you flew in
> the messenger of hope

Few of the poems start with sad tones but gradually come back to normal state.God's feathery touch is there to change the situation.Smt. Shobhaji tries to locate herself somewhere in the atmosphere, feel it internally and express that feeling, that realization in her select words, which appear themselves as musical notes.The poet speaks like Sufi mystics-

> The winter leaf sails
> across the vast expanse of the sky
> has the time come to sail
> into the unknown land?

Prayers can be termed as poems but prayers cannot be called as poems. Poems are essentially related to aesthetic realization.The composition, the rhythm, the sound, the context and the meaning are the basic characters of poetry. Poetry is the celebration of language.It is an expression of vibrant existence, the pain and pleasure of life in total. 'I am the fire' falls in the category of prayer.

> 'Lord let your grace shower on me
> let my soul shine
>
> ....
>
> let me live a pure life' etc.

'I am a gardener'is good but scattered images of the poem may not convey the meaning in its entirety.This is perhaps because of the poet's centered sensibility of her inward journey.She tries to filter down her thoughts into her silent and meditative inner world.Here and there such poems appear.Images sometimes create mental agony and thus the thought process is blocked.

> I hate weakness
> make me strong O' Lord
> I need your grace
> to complete my journey.....
> and when my flapping wings tire
> I will find my Lord waiting for me
> at the golden gate.

Such lines create the crucial images, which simply console the mind.'Between you and me,' 'Goodbye', 'I don't see myself', 'In search of'and few other poems are the product of a very mature mind. In 'Space' the poet plays with her words and feelings. The major images with their classical aura such as sun, moon, sky, sea become soul searching tools. She does'nt allow others to participate in the game of life.Why?Is it for her salvation?Everyone knows that it is impossible to solve the puzzle of life and death.I feel these poems are not of drawing room writings.They are all out in the vast world, but ultimately this world dissolves itself in the mind, body and soul.

The poet is not very much concerned with the present society.It is true that a poet is not a social reformer, politician or a religious leader.She does not try to define the world, she simply accepts it as it is.The happenings in the outside world inspires her to react…words have very limited meaning. They are incapable of communicating the real meaning.The words have to interact with other words, then the meaning emerges through the space which is left between them.The poet knows the importance of space.Every poem has got it's space.The love which is there with it's sublime beauty is 'Love Divine'- it is not of 'love profane'.The visual images which are here for expression slowly merge into the silent light of meditation.Meditation is an effort to reach the inner silence. The inner silence is the base for abstract realization.

The Preface which the poet has written clearly indicates her source of creativity, her vision of life.Her space is charged with love and peace. The constrained expression helps to visualize the world in a different way.That is the beauty of her poems.

With best wishes

Shri. Chandrakant Kusnoor

Bio data

Shri Chandrakant Kusnoor

October 21 1931

Qualification –	Masters in Hindi
	Bachelor in Education
Profession -	Professor in Hindi
	Worked in Kannada and Cultural
	department as Assistant Director
Literary work -	Multi lingual poet, dramatist and Artist
	Writes in four languages- Hindi,
	Kannada, Urdu and Marathi
	60 Dramas,6 Novels,3 Short Stories and
	few translations
Awards -	Award from Karnataka Sahitya Academy
	Award from Lalita Kala Academy for his
	Plays and Novel
	Award from Karnataka Nataka Academy
Hobby-	Painting Exhibition held in Bangalore,
	Mysore, Mumbai, Delhi and Kolkatta

Foreword no 2

Invisible threads-A fountain of mystical strains

Indeed it was a very pleasant experience to eye through and contemplate in tranquility-pithy, crispy, short and neatly composed poetic reflections on phenomenon from microcosm to macrocosm penned down by Mrs. Shobha Kulkarni, a sincere teacher and a tenderhearted sentimental woman and a creative bilingual writer.

Most of the poems which are pure meditations on several issues and affairs of the cosmos such as individual soul's journey through earthly life, relationship between jiva(devotee) and the Divine kinship between the Atman and it's dwelling place i.e. human body, body's affinity for and attachment with worldly bindings etc. abounds in metaphysics.

Hymns of the collection namely 'Moksha', 'In search of', 'At your lotus feet', 'My soul is weak', 'Has the time come','path of spirituality', 'between you and me' comprise mystical strains or strands.Mysticism is supposed to be a path or approach to reach and to be united with the Godhead. Seeker of truth in the initial stage of his/her sojourn to the Divinity admits his/her weaknesses and endeavours with a single pointed confidence to give up or to get rid of vices, to be pure and virtuous.Such a stage in mysticism is called a purgative stage.The soul that attains purity sets to perceive the presence of Grace around and in itself.Such perceptions and subtle experiences of celestial ephemeral are presented in the collection of poems which the poet rightly calls, 'Invisible threads'.

Life that the individual soul leads is a dream and the soul waking up in reality after Death is enchantingly conceptualized or versified in the lines, 'I dont see myself ...shadow too disappears','I bid goodbye to mother......I feel light and fly', 'the radiance of the full moon touch my inner core' 'I cherish my new found freedom', '....soft music all the way... I am surprised I never heard this music before'. Devotees's imagination as to what may happen after soul is released from the bodily attachments is not only fanciful but also exhilarating.

Most of the confessions, decisions and longings of the 'dark night' of the soul expressed in the poems have correspondence with the ideas contained in the metaphysical poems of the British poets and devotional poetry of Hindi and Kannada saints.

Poet who is an excited devotee in the poems looks down on the worldly lures and allurements to look up at the Divinity, for mere discard or hatred for the worldly hardships, miseries does not enable the devotee to establish union with the Ultimate; she will have to seek the assistance of the Invisible Spirit and such yearning is beautifully and aptly expressed in the poem,'My soul is weak'.

Along with the help of God, guidance of the spiritualists who have mystical experiences or those who have traversed the paths of spiritualism is also sought by the devotee to scale the lofty height of Divinity.

Devotee in the poems seeking the help of fire and water for purification, fire for burning sins and water for washing away impurities has it's correspondence with Donne's 'Batter my heart' and Basavanna's host of Vachanas.Along with devotional poems the poet has also written secular poems like, 'The world in a mess' 'Empty boats' and 'The Chair' in which an element of satire and irony is prominent and they show the chaotic situation of the present world in a compact style.

Poet's style of infusing maximum information in minimum words and intensity of feelings deserve a superlative 'superb'. The study of her poems gives the readers an experience of the pilgrimage. I wish her all the best.

Dr. Gurudevi Huleppanavarmath

Lingaraj College BELGAVI

Shobha Kulkarni

Dr.Gurudevi U. Huleppanavarmath
Associate Proffesor of English
KLE Lingaraj College, Belgavi
Eminent Bi-lingual writer
Has published collection of poems-My Voice
Metaphysical Poetry and Kannada Vachana Literature
A study in comparision
Member of - International school of Dravidian Linguistics
            Indian Association for English Studies
            Indian Association for American Studies
She is also a member of many other organisations

PREFACE

Our whole Universe, everything in space, the whole cosmos is invariably connected with invisible energy, love and faith. Some feel it while others don't. Some understand the depth of this invisible energy and some remain insensitive to everything and everyone around them. Art need not alienate you from the crowd. Being sensitive to everyone's feelings itself is a huge positive step towards peace and love which alone can give a real meaning to life. Reading or writing poems can give a new meaning to life every moment. A writer enjoys lot of freedom while putting forth his ideas and thoughts. I would like to quote Franz Kafka, 'A piece of literature must be an axe for the frozen sea inside us'.

I don't know what intelligent writing is nor the yardsticks for measuring it. I always look within me and find answers for my queries. If at all I look outside me it is only Nature, my jasmine twines twirling around the iron bars, the pure white jasmines waiting to wish me. When this tiny jasmine can spread fragrance of love and faith in the world why can't we do the same? My curious money plant climbing higher up on the other side of the fence and the pretty yellow, white and red blossoms, the butterflies and the birds give immense pleasure. Sometimes the sleepy roads wake up late in the night to say 'hi' to me. The roads, the milestones all fascinate me. It reminds me that Life is after all a journey towards some unknown destination. Meditation alone helps me in understanding where I stand. When I leaned on Mother Earth and begged her for courage to complete my sojourn, she said, 'don't lean on me my child, it hurts; you are the atom, you are the Universe, you are the source of energy within, you are the courage you seek in others be brave my child, do not lean on me, it hurts.' Many a rough terrain have I treaded but with Lord's name on my lips I have crossed all hurdles. The sea seems to be larger than life but when the waves come and touch my feet I feel the oneness with the sea itself. Every drop of water in the ocean has a story to tell, the saga of human beings. My thoughts and words may not be perfect but I've tried. I persistently try to connect to something within me, I don't know what to name it. Some say it's Atma but I really don't know.

A moment comes in everybody's life when every relation seems meaningless. Everyone seems to have deserted you. You are alone, all alone but this is the exact moment when you grow tall. If you courageously face this moment, you find soulmates and then Life's sojourn becomes joyous and meaningful. I hope the reader can feel and enjoy the invisible energy while going through this collection.

> my poems are nothing
> but droplets
> on the lotus leaves
> ready to slip back
> into the stream.
> the balancing act
> is tiresome for the drops
> like me; I'm tired

> too tired
> ready to slip back
> into my home
> my real home.

Indeed it is true that a writer has to tread unknown paths and create her own landscapes through her imagination and give an extraordinary touch to an ordinary event.

Shobha Kulkarni

Empty boats

fading sunlight
empty boats
tired hungry fishermen
back on the sandy shore.
can the salty sea
quench their thirst?
can the rocky island
ever satiate their hunger?
the receding waves bid goodbye
to yet another day of toil
shallow words
empty minds
can they ever fathom
the depth of truth?
the sparklers in the sea
are not for all to see.

Kshamaya Dharitri

Who says I'm not touched
by man's sorrow?
didn't I embrace Sita
in her sorrow?
millions have been slaughtered
in what men call 'war'.
did I raise my voice in anger?
sorrow rains on me.
agony of poverty amidst plenty,
hatred amidst love,
willful cruelty of man,
jilted lovers,
sodden souls,
the war in them,
the pride in them,
is all reflected on the sole that tread on me.
yet, every moment
I whisper soothing words.
who says I have become immune
to atom bombs and human bombs?
I wriggle in pain
but bear I must
to respect the label stuck on my forehead,
'Kshamaya Dharitri'.
my beloved,
the canopy on my head
with all his celestial bodies,
finds it difficult to smile radiantly.
the clouds of sadness
sail across his vast expanse,

thundering,
flashing lightning in anger,
wanting to reduce you to ashes,
but because he loves me so......
he lets the sun shine
and I continue to carry your burden,
promising you nothing
about morrow
promising you nothing
about morrow.

Kshamaya – All forgiving
Dharitri – earth
Sita – character from the epic Ramayana

So near yet so far

amidst
towering skyscrapers
I live in a hole
called home
I know no school
for life's my school.
I sell odd things
on the pavement
Oh the rich bargain a lot.
rich creamy temptations
melt around me
eyes gobble up
everything that's free
my hands burn
in my empty pockets
so near yet so far.
as dusk sets in
I lie under the canopy
of luminous stars
and wrap myself
in starry dreams
so near yet so far.
a place of worship near by
Idols shining
heads bowing
so near yet so far.

The world in a mess

It's you and I
who've created this mess
we have but none to blame.
loads are heaped on skeletal backs
darkened by the scorching sun.
cups and saucers
in tender hands
ready to crash and break.
fragile figures
walking miles…
for a drop of water.
adamant religious heads
failing to see the light of science
dragging us back towards darkness.
power in the wrong hands
creating havoc everywhere.
a bomb here
a bomb there
world a slaughter house.
It's you and I
who've created this mess
we have but none to blame.

An Even Song

standing
on the threshold of even
having spent
a long summer day
of blazing heat,
having prayed noisily
I now wait
for some ephemeral clouds
to trap me
like they trapped
the incandescent sun
and transformed him
into an entity
of love and serenity.
the evening star
waits
with it's luminous aura
to touch my soul
but
the fear of a cyclonic wind
still lingers on.
will it destroy everything?
as I gaze
beyond my window pane
praying silently
to the source of life,
I only hope
that it's fragrance
would fill the air
like the fragrance

of the jasmine buds.
what more do I have to share
when dusk has set in
and the vibrant colours of the day
are ready to bid adieu?
as the winged ones too
stop chirping
and curl their necks
in the warmth of their nests,
I too spread my bed
for yet another cold night.

Moksha

When the waves
beat the rocks
I pity them
how helpless they are
against the onslaught
of the tidal waves.
today I know
they willingly give themselves up
to the forceful buffeting of the waves
which smoothen their ridges so…
why cant we willingly give ourselves up
to the divine force
to mould us as He wishes?
When the first rays of sunshine
touch the snow capped mountains
melting them
I pity them
how harsh the sun…
but I'm astounded
to see the glaciers
dancing and flowing in streams
sprinkling love and joy.
why cant we do the same
melt our ego
and sprinkle love and joy?
when the autumn wind
shake and rattle
the last leaf and blossom
in the greenwood
I pity them

for not being able to hold them firmly
close to their bosom with love and care.
but now I see
a new meaning in it all.
the trees are wise
they know the ways of life.
to shed their crowning glory
is to shed all attachments.
why cant we do the same?
shed all worldly attachments
and wait for the Almighty?
wait for Moksha?

Moksha – Liberation

In search of

In search of
soft breezy words
I walk amidst the sea of people
hurrying to and fro
muttering all the time.
In search of
the beauty of silence
that can make mockery of words
I traverse along the sylvan woods
and embrace the trees of knowledge.
In search of
oneness with the oceanic tides
and the empyrean sky
with it's luminaries
I walk along the sandy shore
gazing at the horizon.
In search of
light
for my flickering wick
I tread along the coast of truth
and move from shrine to shrine.
light
eludes me
my search continues
last life
this life
and may be
next life.

My voice

My voice
has already reached
it's destination
in the bards home
of yester years.
tomorrow my voice
may sing no more
the melancholy
or the joys of the crowd.
the world will find
new voices
new faces
to sing the eternal song
of human saga
in new tunes.

Come what may

Come what may
the cuckoo sings
and heralds the spring.
come what may
the thousand eyed peacock
spreads it's feathers
to welcome the nectar of heaven.
come what may
the blooming florets
paint the world
and the winged ones
sing their melodious tune.
come what may
the blazing heat
of the incandescent sun
burn our galaxy.
come what may
the dead are burned
and ashes collected
the urn of the loved ones
float to a distant land.
come what may
life goes on.

I don't see myself

slowly
as I
watch myself
I'm stunned
I don't see
myself
anywhere
my shadow too
has disappeared
with the
sinking sun
leaving
only painful
memories
rising higher
and higher
in the sky
becoming
one with
the grey clouds
sailing
across the sky.
I
sky
my pain
become one.

Goodbye

I bid goodbye
to Mother
I feel light and fly
in the open sky.
where have all the birds gone
I wonder
or maybe I can see
no more without
my body
but I can feel the
presence
of so many things
around me
or maybe
I'm imagining
I can feel no more
without my body.
everything
comes to a full stop
nothing remains
this is life
this is death
this is life after
death.

Between you and me

Between you and me
a strange bird
flaps it's wings
dives into the sea
it mesmerises me.
from a distance
the sails beckon me
makes me restless
reminds me
of the journey
through land
through air
through water
to strange destinations.
the bird comes back
frees me from all bonds.
the sails
have messages
written all over them
the boat of spirituality
not afraid
of mighty
haughty waves
trying to tilt it
destroy it.
courage alone can show
you the path
I stretch my hands
for helping hands
but no,

the journey
is yours they say.
I walk on the water
plunge into the boat
the soul's journey
on strange waters
does not leave
a trail behind
for others to follow.
only
in the silence
of your mind
you can see
the trail
the shore
light.
my tryst
with You has begun
my life
on earth has ended.

Roaring waves

I was born
with the sound of
the roaring waves
beating my eardrum.
my body soaked
in the salty sea
and rolled on the golden sand.
my ancestors have survived
the rains
the storms
the heat and hunger
but I've deserted them all.
I've travelled
miles and miles away
set my own world
smile
pretend to be happy.

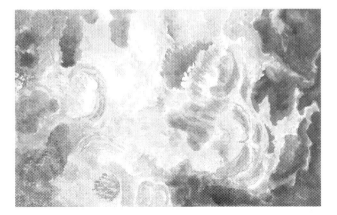

At your lotus feet

Lord
I've come
to offer
my burden
I've dropped it
at your lotus feet
please accept it
make me light and free
I'm alone
in this forest
I know not the path
I stand still
not knowing
which way to go
death hides behind
one of those bushes
I know not
when it will
pounce on me.
let Thy name be
always on my lips
Lord
I ask you not for more.

Love

Love?
what is it I ask the bare tree
staring at me.
I move further
see the squirrels darting
past me
in search of the hidden nuts
memory fails
they starve
on that cold winter morn.
you die
I die
die to everything
dull and cold
wait for the sleepy sun
to awake.

Turmoil

I walk in too many worlds
and I've worn
too many faces.
I try to destroy them all
to find my true self.
dissolve I must
all differences
and end my turmoil
before the winged ones
curl their neck
for a long slumber.

Emptiness

I am the
emptiness
in your life.
you filled your life
with the essence
from the jasmines
around you
and roamed freely
while I
lived
with this emptiness
growing
everyday
till
I become
emptiness
and
lost to the world.

Autumn

my feet trample
the dry twigs
the autumn leaves
strewn on the path
wrapping the Mother Earth.
has autumn
set in a little too soon?
trying to engulf my limbs?
still my grey matter?
whatsoever
till my last breath
your beauty will entice me
your autumn leaves
is a tribute
to my last rites.
I thank thee
for being with me
this last autumn.
the difficult moment
will soon pass away
my soul will fly
across the vast empyrean sky
with your autumn leaves.
when my flapping wings tire
I'll find my Lord
waiting for me
at the golden gates.

My soul is weak

I've reached
the evening of my life
my soul is weak
how can I complete my journey?
on either side
souls move
they are strong
they know the way
I'm weak
Lord, why did you make me weak?
I hate weakness
make me strong O Lord
I need you're grace
to complete my journey.

Path of spirituality

Burn yourself
on the path of spirituality
you are alone,
all alone
as you tread this path.
fear not, oh heart
some unseen force
is always there
to hold your hand
remove the thorns
that have pricked your sole.
some unseen energy
is always there
to quench
your thirst and hunger.
the chirping of the birds
has silenced
my turbulent mind
the energy that has sweeped
within me
will sustain me
till I reach you
O lord.

Sound and Silence

You exist
between
sound and silence
mind
accustomed
to sound
scared of
movement
of thoughts
in the silence
of the dark hours.
fear of reality
of relationships
to see life
in the lifeless eyes
to see
movement
in the stillness.

Twilight hour

The hurried flapping
of wings
groping in darkness.
a long row of ants
crawling on the wall.
obscure
tedious
path.
the world too noisy
shrewd
cunning.
the serenity of dusk
has drowned
into the depth
of the ocean.
only
the sibilant sound
and the violent dance
of the waves
at this twilight hour.

The song is my soulmate

The radiance
of the full moon
touch my inner core
scribble a song
and disappear
beyond
the yonder mountains…
for days after
the song
is my soulmate
my heart is
full of love
and peace.

I am a garden

I dig
several places
plant saplings
expecting
blossoms
and
lingering fragrance.
nothing happens.
I now dig
within me
sow seeds
of love and warmth
water it tenderly
with
prayer of hope.
someday
I'll have
blossoms
of love
faith
lingering fragrance.

Light Light Light

Light, Light, Light
touch my heart
Light me
Darkness blinds me
What can I achieve in darkness?
I dash all stumbling blocks
and only make noise.
noise deafens me
I cant hear Krishna's flute
and heavenly Omkara
connecting my soul
to the Eternal.
light light light
please touch my heart
and light me.

I am the fire

I am the fire
I am the matter
to be
burnt alive
in the fire
and I am the one
to be purified
to be born
again and again.
every minute
every day
the gross matter
surrounding my soul
should be burnt
or else
it will burn me
then I'll be
as good as dead.
Lord
let your grace
shower on me
let my soul
shine.
let me not
invite
the dead moments
to envelop my soul
let the dead
be dead.
let me live

a pure life.
Lord let
moments
of realisation
touch me
purify me
let each moment
be joy
peace
if my suffering
can bring
love
back into my life
let me burn
but please
be with me O Lord.

Light is Light

Light cannot be
bound by form
can it?
light is light
why bother about form?
all that is needed
is light to
light the dark path.
foolish people
have bound him
in forms
in various prayer houses.
light fills the Universe
pray
it will descend on you
you become the light
and spread everywhere.

Has the time come?

As life's time ticks
the word time
changes it's meaning.
has the time come?
fear of the unknown destiny
sends shivers down my spine
has the time come?
the rocky hills
the snowy mountains
the ocean
the rivers
the lakes
has the time come
to bid adieu?
the swan in the pristine lake
is still enjoying it's ride
on the waves
will it flap it's wings
and fly away
far far away
to a no-return land?
the drop
at the tip of the leaf
has to fall one day
be one with the Mother Earth.
has the time come?
the winter leaf sails
across the vast expanse
of the sky
has the time come
to sail into
an unknown land?

Light

like a sleepy dog
shakes off
the dry leaves and dust
sticking on it's fur
I shake off all
desires and conventions.
I concentrate
only on the Light,
that faint Light
I had lit in my heart
years back;
the light brightened
I now could see the path
hear
soft music all the way.
I'm surprised
I'd never heard this music before
nor seen the musicians.

mother

Mother
you whisper
we don't heed
pretend
to be smarter
think
we can create
a better world.
we lose
your touch
and lose
the very breath
of our life.
Mother
you whisper
our ego
destroys it all.

My beloved

I've been reduced to ashes
by my very own beloved.
but strange, I'm still alive
which part of me is alive
I don't know.
I see the stars twinkling
above my head
in the darkness of the night
I see the green grass below my feet
in the early morn
I'm surrounded by blossoms
of different hues
the fragrance lingers in my heart.
the trees, the rustling leaves
all send their warmth to me
touch my inner core.
finally I realise
I'm whole
alive and happy.

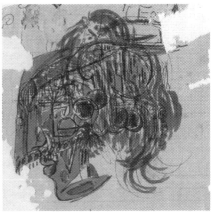

Secret

O mother
you whisper
I'm all ears
you give out the secrets
of life
living
death.
I'm all ears
It's only when I turn
a deaf ear
that you ignore me.
please mother forgive me
forgive my foolishness
and embrace me.
every act of pride
pains you
and me too.
I'll try to give up
everything for you.
I only need your touch
your presence in me
or at least
your assurance
that you are
watching my faltering steps
from somewhere
and you are there
to help me always.

War

war
only a three
letter word
warm bodies
become cold
or worse still
is cut into pieces alive.
every minute
the mind poses the body a question
alive or dead
all parts of the body intact?
how strange
mind and body
must say goodbye
when everything is still green.
why does
mankind impose
death
cruelty
on himself and others
drowning God's gift?

The flame and the curly smoke

the flames of the burning pyre
reach the sky
to bring down some message
I know not what.
the curly smoke
burn my eyes
already wet for the burning body.
a heap of ashes and some bones
is all that is wanted
to be carried in an urn
and merged into the flowing river.
memories etched in my mind
could not be thrown
into the flowing river.
year after year
they rush back and touch
my feet
like the waves
on the beach
I simply stare at the horizon.

Pain

A poet's pain is deep
just like the ocean's depth.
a poet's thoughts
cannot be predicted
just like the wind's direction.
from a grain of sand
from a dewdrop
from a single note of melody
it takes birth, grows
absorbs everything
the pain of the hungry
the pain of the body and mind
pain of separation
the joy of dawn and dusk
the blooming buds
the roaring crystal drops
everything is canvas for the poet
to paint his poem
till his last breath.

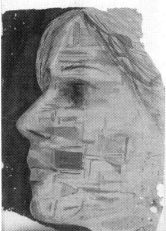

I'm a timeless path

I'm a timeless path
strewn with
autumn leaves
yellow, red and brown
autumn has come
on it's own
the leaves
have embraced
me on it's own
some are peaceful
others are not.
I console them all
the good, the bad and the ugly
all tired wanderers
they fall on me like dead bodies
or are they dead?
some come to me old and tired
some young but defeated
some mission completed
some incomplete
some make life complex
and die too in the same way
difficult it is to understand
the saga of human beings
love
life
twisted like the twirls in the woods
like the smoke
from the simmering fire in the woods.

I'm a timeless path
strewn with
autumn leaves.
I'm a timeless path.

My new found freedom

I cherish
my new found freedom
which came
from nowhere
one day
I was observing
the flame of a wick
struggling to free itself
as the oil dried up.
in a flash
it struck me
I was not in bondage
all these years
as I had thought.
my soul was free
I only had to dry
all my thoughts
of attachment
and then my soul
could take a huge leap
towards the vastness
of the sky
towards
Eternity.

Am I indifferent?

folks think that I'm indifferent
but I'm not; I feel deeply
for all
it's the same
for the folks on the street
for the flapping wings
around me
for the darting squirrels
for the precious blossoms
and the autumn leaves.
for the tidal waves
and the boatmen
for the idols
and the shining lamp
for the babies blue eyes
and their chuckles
for the whispering wind
and their secrets
for the dainty blade of grass
for the enticing look
of the lovers
for the lilting music
and the sonorous voice
touching the sky
for the artists
flight of imagination
the beat of the drum
the sound of the flute
all help me
feel the inner joy

feel the fresh air
and the fragrance of light
you don't see light
you feel light
and feeling
has fragrance of love
and then you willingly
surrender to that
Eternal light
you walk on as though
mesmerized
towards that light.
now tell me
am I indifferent?

Ice cubes

Mother Earth
no bard has described
your beauty
to the fullest
for words
become numb
like ice cubes
in a glass of apple juice
I'd ordered.
I'd to wait
for them to melt;
now I have to
wait eternally
to be able
to scribble
a few lines
on your
breathtaking
beauty.

I'm waiting

I'm a timeless path
waiting
for the autumn leaves
yellow red and brown
to embrace me
to be consoled by me.
sooner or later
autumn comes
it's painful
but the inevitable happens.
mother earth
welcomes
all pain and joy
no grumbling
no rumbling
I see divinity
in mother earth.

Burial

the glittering
spark of muse
was almost dead
and
elaborate
burial plans
were made
but
you tapped
on my window pane
I opened the door
you flew in…..
the messenger of hope
lit the dark streets
of my mind
merged my world
with theirs
and theirs
their joy and misery
the merging
brought
love
peace
poems.

Dusky world

every minute
painful voices shriek
someone
coughs cancerous pain
which roll like marbles
and hit the walls.
turbulence runs high
within the four walls
living through this dusky world
we forget
what love and care is.
we stink and look
like moth eaten leaves
yet beam
with powdered faces
gaudy attire
and dance to the tune
of loud music
bellowing
from some inn.
in the smoky air
of the drawing room
greed lust dance
wine flows
on the red carpet
all leeches here.
as darkness
pours from the sky
cats and dogs
chase each other.

a baby yells for more milk
tugging
at the sapless mother's breast.
the racing mind
cannot fathom
the depth of the Vedas.
not all drops
can balance on the lotus leaf
some fall back
into the stream of tamas, don't they?
can God's soft feathery touch
change everything?

Reflection

I couldn't see
my own reflection
when myriad cracks
appeared on the mirror
and psychological memories
created strange patterns
on it; love simmered
into pain.
I moved away
from my loved ones
and myself too.

The chair

I love the chair
the ebony wood
the carved hands
the long graceful legs
competing with the ladies.
It's a little high
so that I can
look down upon others.
It's spacious
so however bulky I grow
I can sit comfortably.
It's powerful
when I sit
others stand
some with files
some without.
I've framed Gandhi's photo in gold
and hung it behind my back
so that I need not feel
uneasy at his stare.
there are some other leaders too
all in golden frame
they might inspire some souls
but that's not my botheration.
I only like the clinking sound of coins
and rustling sound of notes
under the beautiful chair
I love the chair
I love the chair
It's cozy and warm.

Gandhi – national leader of India

Life

Life
a fabricated net
woven by silken threads
by the eternal weaver
with threads of joy.
those that heed him
joy forever.
those with ego
tamper with the weaving
weave
their own design
of sorrow.

Dust

I don't like tears
they're salty
but these walls
are full of turbulence
sounds deafening.
words burn like hot coal.
men of falsity
deceive me.
warmth
disappears
under the carpet.
I stroll in the garden
caress the soft petals
I look at the dust
settled on the green foliage
and console myself, one day
I too will turn into dust, then
will it matter
who made me cry?
mother earth doesn't
differentiate between the dust
of a dog
or a human being.
we are all one
in her embrace.

Jasmines

I bask in the warmth
of the rising sun
warmth of the kitchen
sizzling hot coffee
the warmth of familiar voices
and the energy
of my Lord.
I feel light
when I inhale the fragrance
of the jasmines in my garden.
with a light heart
I step out
into the indifferent world
nothing shakes me
nothing hurts me
I expect nothing
for I find everything
within me.

I'm a nomad

I'm a nomad
for I was born
in many a womb
cradled by many hands
spent my life
under many roofs
buried or burnt in
many a places.
let that be O Lord
suffice if you
now free me
from all
births and deaths.

Fire

I must create my own fire
I must burn in my own fire
I myself must burn
my own impurities
I myself
must purify myself
I, fire and impurities
are not different
the ashes must flow
in the Ganges
and I must be born again
from the ashes.
dry ash
wet water
birth again
in the land of wisdom.

Ganges –holy river of the Hindus

Feel the words in your heart

I know
where the muse
was born
deep
in the Mother's womb.
you pull her out
drag her
towards the market place
try to sell her there
you want a poem
about them all.
you pull her
to the warfront
show her horrifying scenes
pen down
a couple of lines.
you pull her into
the pretentious flashy crowd,
the assembly of intellectuals
satirical poems are born.
how callous
indifferent
you are within
you truly
never feel anything
you want

inner realisation
light
never realising
you must
feel the words
in your heart first
then in your head.

East and West

The east have the notion
they know
the secrets of life and death.
the west have the best in
science and technology
the young lift their head
but are not sure
whether they'll see
raindrops
or bombs
pouring on them.

Divine light

when
I don't even know
if the seeds
I throw
in my garden
will sprout
how will I know
what divinity is?
may be
thousands of prayers
be born in my heart
for the seeds of light
to sprout.

The little girl

I am the sea
I am the roaring waves
I am the little girl
rolling on the golden sand
and building castles.
God alone knows
how many I've built
and how many
have been washed away
by the tidal waves;
but the little girl
was always happy
collecting shells.
but she grew up…
and she was never heard
giggling
laughing
and dancing again
with the roaring sound of the waves.

Before I bid farewell

I stand
with a brush in my hand
vibrant colors wait to dance
on my empty canvas
my hands tremble a little
for I want it to be the best
before I bid farewell to all.
I sit
with a pen in my hand
sheets of snow white paper
and racing thoughts and words
but my hands tremble a bit
for I want it to be the best
to bid a thankful goodbye to all.
I sit
with a veena in my hand
and ragas in my mind
my voice trembles a little
for I want it to be my best
to bid a farewell to all.
before I end
my cerebration with life
and celebration
with words colors and sound
I struggle to give the best
to the world
before I bid a farewell to all.

Fear is my shadow

A drop of water I am
on a lotus leaf my Lord
slippery like eel
are my thoughts
and fear is my shadow.
time and again I slip
into the stream of tamas.
save me lord
from this flood
of thoughts within me.

Soaked clothes

where is the beginning
where is the end
for the thought process?
thoughts
heavy like the soaked clothes
I cant even lift them
and hang them on the wire.
I give up.
I retreat from this field
of life, love wetness.
I would like some sunshine
dry the linen
make it light light light
fly in space
freedom from myself
my other self
trying to drown me
alive.

The rag picker

Her day begins early
she walks in dignity
with a lose cloth bag
hung on her shoulder
and rummage
through the dustbin
for plastic and other odd things.
my heart aches
to see her thus
but then how am I
different from her?
I too rummage
through the dustbin
of my mind
in search of sparklers
in search of truth.

Thoughts

the awakening
of thoughts
in the cold early morn
boiled in the heat
of the long afternoon hours
to fade away
in the confusion
of dusk
and sink
in the darkness
of night.

Ocean of Ignorance

the racing mind
cannot fathom
the depth of Vedas
not all drops
can balance
on the lotus leaves
some fall back
into the stream of tamas
don't they?
those that balance
shine like beacon lights.
those that slip
drown
into the ocean of ignorance
and are caught
in the whirlpool
of birth and death.

Tamas – lower qualities

Shadow

When the earth
curls for a slumber
darkness smiles.
swirling fan above my head
whispering shadows around me
confusing paths to choose.
streaming light
two snow white winged ones
appear
dance in my mind.
the criss cross paths disappear
the shadows stop whispering.

Why dream?

Why dream
when there's no dreamland
to unfold your wings
and fly in freedom?
why dream
when the connecting string
to the dreamland
and the world of reality
has snapped into pieces?
people ask
why waste time
in the world
of rainbow colors
and words?
when the world of pleasure
beckon some
hunger torture others
dreams coil and sleep.

Sinking Sun

It was already there waiting for me
even before I was born
the pain
the sorrow
the separation
the agony
joy eluded me
It was not for me to dance or laugh
sorrow rained on me
my eyes wet
nothing visible
only unbreakable
cobwebs
around me.

Pancha Bhoota

I'm scared
at the strength of Agni
it can burn papers, dry leaves
houses, jungles
dead bodies
and live women for dowry.
I marvel
at the strength of water
it cleanses, purifies
but sometimes
showers it's angst on living beings
destroying thousands of lives.
Wind astounds me
with it's softness sometimes
but when angry
uproots everything.
the canopy above my head
pours nectar
but when man interferes
brings flood and calamity.
Dharitri
the cynosure of all eyes
rumbles when disturbed
thirsts for human lives.

pancha bhoota – five elements of Nature
Agni – fire, water, wind ,sky,dharitri - earth

My voice has been silenced forever

Bend like a reed
they stamp on you
stand stiff like a tree
they call you proud
cut your limbs
pull out the roots
and threaten you.
I raised my voice
so they buried me alive.
I already feel suffocated
I'll soon lie down
with my values
as my pillow.

A drop of water

A drop of water I am
born deep in the womb
of the mountains
I flow with the other drops
I may join the sea
or evaporate half way
it all depends on the Almighty's plan.
I may gather wisdom on the way
and flow crystal clear
or get tainted
by the pollution around.
it all depends on the path I choose
and the Almighty's plan.
I continue my sojourn
though old and weak now
to join the mighty ocean.

Time is stubborn

I didn't want past
to build my present
and future steps
but time is stubborn
it darts like a fish
through
past
present
future
mix everything
on the canvas of my life.
not that I don't enjoy
the sight
of blooming buds
from the seeds
that I sowed yesterday
I do remember
the icecream sticks
that I licked yesterday
and the next moment
holding it for my child
time melts too quickly
but I didn't want time
to carry
all those heavy thoughts
and burden my back
please don't do this to me

and yes
your hurried footsteps
is too much for me
my grey hair
shivering body
cannot
keep pace with you.

Golden shore

what my mind sees
comes back to me
what my eyes sees
evaporates
like dewdrops
in sunshine
what my mind hears
reverberates in my ears
what my ears hear
is just noise
what imprints I see
in my innermost mind
remains forever
guides me forever
but my footprints
on the sands of time
are wiped away too soon
by the tidal waves.
when the golden shore
is visible
nothing matters
no one matters
for all know
the last journey
has no company.

Tsunami

there's a tsunami
within all of us
devastating our
emotional ties
destroying all
security milestones
on our life's path
washing away
everything.
the bareness
around
mock at us
as we take
faltering steps
on a foggy day.
It takes years
to recover
to smile
and walk ahead
as though
nothing
has happened.

Space

I used to yell
I want space
please don't encroach
my space.
suddenly I feel space
lot of space
I walk freely
I even run freely
yes, nobody can give you space
you have to create it yourself
live for yourself too
I find peace in my space
I stop blaming others
for encroaching my space
I cherish my new found space
I can feel the vast expanse
of the sky
I can hear the temple
and church bells chime
I meditate upon your formless self
and become formless too.
I'm no longer the body
nor my mind
I'm just the formless space.
I no more prepare masks for myself
to be worn at different times.
when I meet people
they are scared of my naked glance
but I have nothing to hide from anyone.
I'm free in my space
and I carry this space everythere.

without mask
my expression
is one and the same for all
whatever I eat
whatever I wear
I don't feel any difference
yet I'm not indifferent
To anyone, anything.
this new found space
dissolves all differences
every minute, every second
every word uttered and heard
from all and sundry
So I live peacefully
another hundred years
a harmless life
full of peace and love.
now life living death
is all same for me
I only see perfection
everywhere
In everybody's words
lines and colors.
I sometimes wonder
what would I do
if I had not found this space
I would be only rolling
around in vicious circles
miserable and lonely.
see, now I have a song in my heart
a tune on my lips
rhythm in my lines.
people say I've changed
but I see the same wrinkles

on my aging face
it's only my new found space
that has changed me.
the ground was already prepared
long ago. without realising
each day I had removed
weeds from my mind's garden
and before I could turn back
and see the clean surface
space had occupied it
and now it does not allow
any weeds to grow.
enough of everything
I hear my inner voice shout
enough of everything
live like a holy spirit
with colors
yet without colors
pure serene
formless
let them all see your light
not your body
let even your aging mother
not recognize you
you have a different story to tell her
and to others
not the one they want to hear
but the words you want to utter
those harmless words
without thorns
pricking none
for this is what space does to you
and to all who truly aspire
light.

Invisible threads

invisible threads
in life's shimmering tapestry
are all woven
into a pattern.
it connects
the fluttering leaves
above my head
the autumn bed
below my feet
the stars
the moon
the oceanic tides
glued to the sea
the miniscule sand
the largest rock
everything
binds together
form a beautiful collage.
Invisible threads
holding
everything
everyone
in the Universe
my thoughts
your thoughts,
nature's music
floating in the air.
the flute you play
your melodious raga
pulls an invisible string

of my heart.
the dead
the alive
are all together
the dead
do not die
they only change forms
and walk with you.
the roots
yes the invisible roots
I soon must grow
roots
of universal connectivity
that's my last wish
and this my last verse
to bid farewell
to the beautiful world
beautiful people
beautiful minds.

Printed in the United States
By Bookmasters